GBEMINIYI EBODA

ACCELERATE YOUR SUCCESS RATE

Accelerate Your Success Rate
By Gbeminiyi Eboda
Copyright © 2013 Move Your World Int'l

All rights reserved. No part of this book may be reproduced or transmitted in any form by any means, electronic or mechanical, including photocopying and recording, or by any information storage and retrieval system, except as may be expressly permitted by the Copyright Act or by the publisher.

Requests for permission should be made in writing to
Move Your World Int'l
email: info@moveurworld.com
phone: +234 (0)809 827 5777, +234 (0)809 218 8889

ISBN: 978-978-936-062-8

Cover: GreenKnight Solutions.
Cover photograph: Aperture Creative Media.

RECOMMENDATIONS

"Pastor Niyi is a man of focus and his progress is clearly outstanding. God's unction on him will multiply in the years to come."
- Taiwo Odukoya.
Fountain of Life Church,
Nigeria

"The greatest things one could do with one's life is to serve God and serve people, and this is what Pastor Niyi has chosen to do, agreeing with God to be a blessing to humanity. I thank God for his life."
- Sam Adeyemi.
DaystarChristian Center

"One of the most dynamic preachers I have ever seen. His knowledge of scriptures is succinct and his value for excellence is seen everywhere around him. He can only be a gift."
- Tunde Ayeni.
Graceville Christian
Center, Nigeria

"Rev Eboda is a man that knows where he is going. There is a vision burning in his heart, a vision that will be fulfilled."
- Sola Kolade.
Vine Branch Charismatic
Church, Nigeria

"Rev'd Niyi's type is rare; he combines such an extraordinary measure of grace, dexterity in the ministry of the Word, uncommon wisdom and a sincere heart of love for God and His people. To see such combination is rare. I'm so proud of him; I blow his trumpet everywhere I go around the world."

- Victor Adeyemi.
Global Harvest Churches

"God has blessed my husband and I with relationships. In all sincerity, Pastor Niyi and his wife stand out. His type is scarce, He is unusually anointed and intelligent, I wonder if God created another preacher when He created him. God has put on his inside what it takes to feed many."

- Funke Felix-Adejumo.
Agape Ministries, Nigeria

"Rev'd Niyi is one of the most respected in the ministry of 'pulpiteering'. He is a man of unusual gifting, strong and precise call to our generation. He is consistent and I appreciate and celebrate God's wisdom and utterance on his lips."

- Korede Adams.
Masterpiece Assembly, Nigeria

"Rev'd Eboda has been such a great mentor and ambassador that we can look up to particularly in the way he follows God. His spirit of excellence and knowledge of the Word is such an encouragement and inspiration. He is a blessing."

- Aaron T Aaron.
Singer, Songwriter,
Director of Doxazo Record Label, UK

CONTENTS

Introduction — ix

1. Celebrating The Individual — 17
2. Unmasking The Negatives — 29
3. Understanding Failure — 39
4. Making A Comeback After A Setback — 47
5. The Power of Knowledge — 59
6. Accelerate Your Success Rate — 67
7. Staying On Top — 81
8. The Challenge Of Success Sustainability — 91
9. Succession Planning — 109
10. Building Spiritual Capital — 117

INTRODUCTION

"Success or otherwise, it's YOUR fault..."

This book of the law shall not depart from your mouth, but you will meditate on it day and night that you may observe to do according to all that is written therein, then you will make your way prosperous and you will have good success."
– *Joshua 1:8 KJV*

The responsibility for your eventuality is at your doorstep. You are the one to ensure that the book of the law does not depart from your mouth; meditate on it day and night, and observe to do according to all that is written therein and then you will make your way prosperous and you will have good success. The 'you' factor, is therefore a critical success factor. Once upon a time, a king had a daughter to give out in marriage, so he sent out the town crier to make the announcement. The required qualification was however not mentioned. All the men who felt they had the prospect of becoming the king's son-in-law showed up. When they assembled, the king told them it was easy to become his son-in-law; all they had to do was to swim across a river. The river was not a very long one – about fifty meters. The only problem was that it was infested with crocodiles!

Becoming the king's son-in-law was a fantastic idea, but the price was a no-go area and no one was willing to risk his life, embarking on such a venture. All the men stood at the brink of the river looking at the prize – the king's daughter, but none could pay the price. One of the men said to another, "You go now."

Replying, he said, "how can I go? I am the only son of my parents. There are three of you in yours."

Another said, "I am the only one who went to school in my family..."

While they were on one side of the river contemplating, they suddenly heard a rumbling in the water. In no time, someone had desperately swum across. Emerging at the other side to a thunderous applause, the young man asked panting, "who pushed me?" It was never his idea to venture into the river – he was pushed!

This book is designed to give you that kind of push. It was written to propel you to 'hug the monster!' Dare the odds and venture the impossible, because the impossible is usually the untried.

Getting the Details

There are four things that will make you get the best out of this book as you read: take, think, teach and try.

You must take notes because the faintest pen is better than the brightest mind or memory. The ability to pay attention to details is a key ingredient for success. Francis Bacon said, "Reading makes for a full man, but writing makes for a detailed man."

You should also think things over. Let your mind function like a window with the ability to open or close. If it cannot be closed, it isn't a window but a hole. If it can't be opened, it is not a window but a wall. It is essential to be able to open and close our minds appropriately and make sound judgments from what we read. Consider what you read "because the Lord will enable you to understand it all." [2]

The capacity to do, is developed in the place of meditation. When you think it through, move on to teaching it, and finally try doing it. We usually forget what we hear; and remember what we teach; but we become what we do. The ultimate proof of knowledge shows up in the development of habits. You don't really know it if it has not become a habit for you. There are many things people say but they don't do. It implies they don't know it yet.

The principle of the critical success factor says certain factors are more responsible for success in an organization than others. These are not factors we share with others; they are factors we shield from them. Those who are leader labels in their industries understand how to use these critical success factors to maintain their monopoly. It gives them the competitive advantage in their trade. The only way to break their monopoly is to access the knowledge that has given them exclusive right to trade dominance.

Not everybody in the field of play is actually involved in the performance. Some are just mobile spectators, running from one end of the field to another. What is the use of your presence if it has no consequence on the outcome of the game? A footballer running from one end of the field to the other without making contact with the ball is a spectator wearing a jersey.

Gaining access to the trade secrets of the leader labels in every industry is a major step at breaking their monopoly. That is why it has been said that the new source of power will not be money in the hands of a few, but information in the hands of many. The 21st century economy is a knowledge-driven one. The only way to create a gap between yourself and the competition therefore is to do an outstanding job with information. That is the way to establish a competitive advantage in a knowledge-driven economy.

INTRODUCTION

There is a place known as the Silicon Valley which is in the Southern part of the San Francisco bay in Northern California; less than 50-mile stretch between San Jose and San Francisco in the United States of America. In 1996, the Silicon Valley produced 44,000 millionaires in dollar terms. Two years later, 120,000 millionaires emerged from the Silicon Valley. The Silicon Valley is the knowledge center of the world. Remember, we get paid for what we know and our relevance is a function of our competence in other people's area of ignorance.

Over the next few pages, we will be going on a mental journey; a journey of wisdom and our principal manual is the word of God because no other person has access to the secrets of good success except God. Your rate of success in life will be directly proportional to your proximity to His presence. For as long as Uzziah sought God, he prospered. You cannot prosper beyond your proximity to His presence. When we seek the Lord, all other things will be added to us. "The young lions suffer and lack but they that seek the Lord will not lack any good thing..." [2]

In Genesis 27:20, a man asked his son, "How come you found it so quickly?" The son answered, "Your God brought it my way." As far as wealth is concerned, before it is acquired, it must be entrusted. So God has to bring it your way because He is the one who gives the power to make wealth; to establish His covenant.

The power to make wealth ultimately comes from God. Wealth creation is a function of power in operation. There is no wealthy man without an altar! Some men don't just lend to organizations; they lend to nations. It is not possible to attain such a status without having an altar. The altar may however be to God or to the devil. The difference is that it is only the blessing of the Lord that can make rich and add no sorrow. This book is packaged with light for flight. He made a light to rule by day, and another by night. Therefore, whether it is in the day or at night, it takes Light to rule!

The strength of the oppressor is always in the maintenance of ignorance. There are people who go to business schools to learn principles that will advance their lives. The principles resident in the word of God will push you ahead of your contemporaries. The kind of wisdom that comes from God is such that men will behold and wonder where it came from.

To get the best out of this book, your mind and your heart have to be involved. Benjamin Franklin said, "Teach me and I will forget; show me and I may remember; involve me and I will understand." The involvement of your mind is very vital because your mind is the seat of reasoning. Your heart also has to be involved because it is the seat of passion and emotions; it is the seat of decisions. If anyone is going to make up his mind to do something, it has to come from his heart.

> **You cannot prosper beyond your proximity to His presence.**

What is the use of knowledge if there is no commensurate application of what has been discovered? Remember, there is a gap between ignorance and knowledge, but there is a wider gap between knowledge and its application. There is blessing, not in the knowing but in the doing. Many people know, but they don't do. They therefore have a "constipation of revelation." We have to commit ourselves to doing. Ezra prepared himself to seek the law of the Lord; to do it and to teach it (Ezra 7:10).

There is a blessing in knowing; a blessing in sharing and a greater one in doing.

chapter one

CELEBRATING THE INDIVIDUAL

chapter one
CELEBRATING THE INDIVIDUAL

"Individuals define organizations and ultimately nations!"

When several products offer similar solutions and price is not a constraint, brand preference is determined by value.

As we begin this journey, it will be ideal to lay a foundation about our values as individuals and why we need to create best-selling brands out of ourselves. To create a brand, one has to develop a momentum of performance. When several products offer similar solutions and price is not a constraint, brand preference is determined by value. Such value could be real or imagined and it is not determined by the perception of the producer, but by that of the consumer.

There are basically two levels of marketing: self-advertising and indirect marketing. In the former case, the creator of the product also projects its image. Indirect marketing is however a higher level of marketing, in which the consumer becomes the advocate of the product. In the market-place, potential consumers assume four possible postures: suspects, prospects, clients and loyalists. We will explore these in further details much later in this book.

It takes exceptional service delivery to transform suspects to loyalists. It has been established that when people go to shop, they don't just shop for products; they also shop for experience. When product or service-delivery falls below customer expectation, there is a potential loss of customers. For every customer lost by a producer, there is a competitor eagerly waiting to relieve him of the burden of relevance. We therefore need to make profitable investments in our service delivery, to sustain relevance.

Your relevance to me would be a measure of your competence in my area of ignorance.

There is no doubt about the fact that we live in a knowledge-driven environment and what employers hire new staff for, is not their looks (except models), but the value they have in-between their ears. Your relevance to me would be a measure of your competence in my area of ignorance. It therefore implies that when you have relevance in an area of ignorance that is critical to me, I will begin to gravitate towards you because you have what I need. It should be a desire in us all that as we progress in life, our names would evolve into becoming addresses for solutions. That is the only way our names will become synonymous with success.

The word 'gates' naturally talks about barriers, but when the name of Bill Gates is mentioned, we don't think of barriers. We rather think of computers and billions! We are in a world of competition and we must make up our minds to become apex personalities. No matter how good you are at what you do, always remember there is another player in the same field who will not relent at making sure he gets a cut of your market share. It is therefore important to maintain cutting-edge relevance.

It is said that when you find someone who enjoys what he does, it is possible that what he does is easy for him. However, I beg to disagree. Loving a task does not mean it is easy. Tiger Woods loves golf, but it is not an easy task for him. It is said that his practice sessions last between 7 to 8 hours in length! So, if you want to become a legendary golfer, you must be ready to swing the club at least a thousand times a day.

There is nothing like status quo in life; everyone is either upwardly mobile or spiraling downwards. Even those who choose to maintain static positions, relative to the movement of others would soon find themselves at the rear because others are not stagnant. The future is not only the opportunity of the poor to become rich; it is also the challenge of the rich to stay rich or get richer.

There are people who were rich in the 70s, but are no longer rich today, because they found themselves being plunged into situations and circumstances for which they were ill-prepared. Maintaining cutting-edge relevance no doubt demands a lot of hard work.

Success may be "sweat-less," but it is never "effort-less." Something has to give way.

The dictionary remains the only place where success comes before work. Success may be "sweat-less", but it is never "effort-less". There is no way a man will achieve success without a measure of effort on his part. Something has to give way. Distractions have to be side-lined. There are certain things that would want to be the audience of your indulgence and there are things that would want to patronize your excesses. You must learn to ignore such enticements. That is the only way to constantly remain in forward motion.

Every developmental growth has four phases:

1. Observation: An awareness of my environment and the models that exist in it.
2. Imitation: This is the paediatrics of development. Children begin to walk because they see other people around them walking.
3. Creation: Every man should strive towards evolving from the phase of imitation to developing his own ingenuity.
4. Identity: At the point of developing your uniqueness, when trying to establish a personal brand, it is normal to be at the receiving end of criticism and cynicism. If you can survive that phase by maintaining a momentum of performance, you will eventually establish your own identity – a signature brand. That is when you become an address for a solution.

A pastor friend shared his experience at a program he attended some years back. To facilitate his entry, he was given a tag and a sticker for his car. So, when he drove into the venue, the protocol officers directed him to a reserved parking lot upon seeing the sticker on his car. When he got out of the car, he had to wear the tag as well, so he could be allowed into the hall. He was given a seat with the ministers, but at the rear end of that section. He however felt good about it because many other people were lost in the congregation.

While he sat there, Pastor E. A. Adeboye walked in wearing a very simple outfit with his trade-mark tambourine and no tag on his cloth. He was ushered all the way to the front row. As a matter of fact, they had to excuse someone who was wearing a tag for the man who was not wearing a tag to sit. There is a phase in life when you are known with a tag, and there is another phase when with or without a tag, your name becomes an address for a solution.

This chapter places a major emphasis on the individual because individuals define organisations and ultimately nations. There was a Swiss man named John Calvin, though originally French, but later migrated to Switzerland. In his days, he called his countrymen together and declared to them that despite the fact that their country did not have natural resources, they would create a resource called "honesty", making it a taboo to do anything shady in the country. They all bought into it and took personal ownership of the vision. Their words became their bond and each man worked towards having oneness to his personality; what a man was in the dark, was what he was in the light.

Over time, the Swiss became known for the manufacture of watches because watches are also symbols of precision. Who has better right to precision than people who are honest and consistent? Beyond the fact that Swiss make the best watches in the world, they are also known for their attention to detail (precision) and respect for time. Thus, there is an inextricable link between precision and respect for time. Most people do not see that link; they are only aware of the fact that the Swiss make the best wrist watches. Swiss watch-making perfection is linked to their precision or attention to details, as well as a sense of the importance of time. The Swiss are usually never late for an appointment!

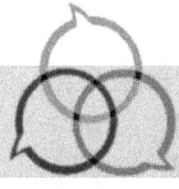

There is an inextricable link between Precision and respect for time.

They were also known for their banking system. This evolved because whatever was left with the Swiss was sure to be kept intact. Today, even treasury-looters in Africa transfer their loot to Swiss banks because they cannot trust their own cronies with their loot. They know that their monies would be safe in Switzerland. It all began with a man who decided that if his nation did not have a natural resource, they would create a nobler resource by making honesty a creed for all to live by.

Someday, corruption infested countries in Africa will celebrate the emergence of a generation of people that will create a resource that will change the face of their nation in the committee of nations. If we come together and agree to do things in the right way, over time, based on the law of sympathetic resonance, we will begin to find more of our kind.

Building Self-worth

Parents and especially fathers are very strategic as far as the future of their children is concerned. Every child is like an arrow in the quiver of the parent. A child will go as far as the parent can shoot him. The job of a father is to ensure that his son or daughter goes farther than he does. As a father, you will be a failure if your child does not improve on your achievements. This is not limited to biological fathers alone; the same rule applies in a mentor-protégée relationship. There are fathers who even envy the success of their children. That is the highest level of insecurity. It should be your joy that your child is an improvement of whatever level you attain. Mothers are also strategic, and that is why it is said that the hand that rocks the cradle also rules the world. I thank God for the things I learnt from my mother, though she has passed on. She taught me industry and enterprise. She taught me how to handle rejection because that is one of the hallmarks of maturity. She taught me to believe in myself.

Because you are not sent to everybody, it should not be your responsibility to want to appeal to everyone.

Not everyone will believe in you, no matter how hard you try because you are not sent to everybody. It should not be your responsibility to want to appeal to everyone. You should learn to be and do your best, and let God do the rest. There are people who have told me they were surprised when they saw me after listening to my messages, because the looks didn't match the utterances! I smile at such comments because a man's status isn't a function of his stature. Your worth is not a function of how tall, short, fat or slim you are. Those statistics are mere variables of least consequence. Your worth is tied largely to your competence which is a function of your knowledge.

Knowledge has both an immediate value and a post-dated relevance. So whether you will use it now or later, what largely matters is how you store it. Do you store it in a way that is easily retrievable? We all need knowledge, because we pay for our ignorance; knowledge and wisdom are vital and non-negotiable.

Anyone who plays truancy from wisdom has automatically registered for crisis and errors!

Wisdom is neither a function of age nor experience. That an individual has been married for 25 years does not qualify him or her to be a marriage counselor. You need to appraise the quality of your own marriage before you can become an authority on the subject of marriage. If you have results, and your methods have worked for you, people can then learn how to do it from you.

The best of God's gifts are still packaged in human form. Unravel the "package" that you are and let the world enjoy the fragrance of His knowledge through YOU!

chapter two

UNMASKING THE NEGATIVES

chapter two
UNMASKING THE NEGATIVES

> "Failure is never final. There can always be a comeback after a setback."

The discovery of purpose helps us to know that we do not need everything in life. Anything we have without a purpose attached to it is in the bracket of excess in our lives.

Negatives in the context of this discourse simply refer to failure. This chapter will examine five myths or misconceptions about failure. Imagine a scenario where you take a look at your career, and it is clearly a failure. Or you examine your performance as a parent or a spouse, and it's an obvious failure. In a subsequent chapter, we will look at the right perspective to failure; how to avoid the ditches; how to make a comeback after a setback; and examples from the lives of those who have been there before and how they evolved out of it.

Myths/Misconceptions about Failure
1. Failure is relative to the success of others. Based on this misconception, some

people measure what they have based on what others have that they don't. It thus becomes a very unbearable scenario when a man doesn't have a car and all his friends have at least one each. He thus sees himself as a failure because his friends have what he doesn't have. That is a misconception.

You don't measure failure relative to the apparent success of others because when you discover purpose, it will free you from the crisis of comparison. The discovery of purpose helps us to know that we do not need everything in life. Asking God for a billion dollars isn't an intelligent prayer. What you need do is to discover the billion-dollar vision in God's heart. When He gives you the vision, He will equip you with the one billion dollars needed to execute it.

Prosperity is having enough of God's resources to accomplish His will for our lives. His will for our lives vary. He called Moses to lead 3.5 million people, while He called Mordecai to raise just one child, who was not even his own. She was his surrogate daughter. He made unquantifiable investments in that girl named Esther and she was strategically positioned at a time the nation needed help.

Moses was raised by his mother in a way that qualified him to be a deliverer of a whole nation. His mother's task was not to lead 3.5 million people, but to raise their leader. There is therefore something about finding your purpose and celebrating it.

Anything we have without a purpose attached to it is in the bracket of excess in our lives. The more we increase the bracket of our excesses, the more we become vulnerable in life.

2. Failure is determined by the opinion of significant others. In life, people generally fall into two categories: those for whom we share sentiments e.g. a spouse, family members or other people for whom we have respect; and those whose influences on our lives are insignificant or entirely inconsequential. The words that the former group speaks into our lives carry a lot of weight. When insulted by another road-user while driving, it is obvious such a person isn't a significant other. Responding to him is simply a waste of valuable time.

However, comments made to us by our significant others can be very weighty. If for example, a wife tells her husband she doesn't believe in him, nothing could be more crushing for a man than that. But failure is not determined by the opinion of even the significant others. The negative opinions of other people about us do not have to become a reality in our lives, irrespective of who they are. How we respond will allow or disallow the fulfilment of such 'prophecies'.

> **What happens to us is never as important as what happens in us.**

3. Failure is what happens to us. Failure at what we do should never be taken as failure in who we are. Many years ago, at the earlier phase of his ministry in the U.K, a notable gift of God hosted a program in which he projected and made provisions for an attendance of about 1000 people. Despite all the publicity done, less than ten showed up. That figure included himself, his wife and two sons. He simply said: "it was the program that failed, I did not".

Today, that same man pastors the largest church in the U.K. If he had allowed that experience to cage him, he would have become a relic of history, and not the man that is being celebrated globally today.

I once read a quote that says, "Success is okay if it does not get into the head; and failure is not so bad if it does not affect the heart." What happens to us is never as important as what happens in us. One of my mentors once shared the story of a man who was found dead in his house.

That the man was found dead wasn't the significant aspect of the story, but the fact that he was found dead with tears in his eyes. He wept out of life into eternity. He gave up; he threw in the towel. Failure isn't what happens to us, it's what happens in us.

4. All failures can be avoided. That is not true. Some failures can be avoided, but not all failures can be avoided. Often times, the avoidance of failure is also the avoidance of success. The path to success is usually laid with speed-breakers which we call "failures".

I also came across a quote that says "Those who see failure as an enemy are usually subservient to those who conquered it; the fellow who never makes mistakes will end up taking orders from the one who does." Selah!

We are not 'human-bes' but 'human beings'.

5. Failure is final. It is not unusual for people to take a snap-shot of our lives and conclude that the moment we fail once, we are permanently failures. Men look at us in pictures but we live our lives in motion. Someone may have met you at a point when you were not your best and therefore draws a conclusion. However, you would have gone from that point to repackage yourself, thereby re-writing your history. But for those people who met you back then, they still define you based on what they saw.

Some years ago, while visiting my in-laws with one of my associate pastors, we saw the picture of what must have been a two-year old girl hung on the wall. My associate asked me who that was, and as hard as I looked, I really couldn't figure out who it was. I asked my mother-in-law, and she said "that was your wife at two." I could not even recognise her. Certainly, someone who last saw her at that age would never identify her if he or she still chooses to locate her with that picture in mind.

A friend of mine was once denied an employment in a particular telecoms firm. It was such a painful experience for him, but he moved on and joined another telecoms outfit where he rapidly rose to a top managerial position. At some point in time, they needed to hire some senior level staff and he was in charge of the recruitment exercise. Lo and behold, one of the applicants was the same man who had denied him a job in the other company, years earlier!

...face value is usually false value.

Someone once said, "We are not 'human-bes' but 'human beings'." A 'human be' suggests rigidity of fate, but being a human being tells us our lives are in continuous tenses. So, you may be poor, but you will not always be poor. You may be a student but someday, you will be the teacher; you may be a child but someday, you will become a parent. Our lives are in motion!

On November 30, 1995, God said to me, "Be careful how you treat people, because you don't know who they are, and where next you will meet them" He told me if I had met Him before He made everything and shook hands with Him, I would have been shaking hands with EVERYTHING without knowing. Face value is usually a false value. Never relate with people by mere sight but with insight because you don't know where they are going. Failure is never final. There can always be a comeback after a setback.

chapter three

UNDERSTANDING FAILURE

chapter three
UNDERSTANDING FAILURE

"Failure is an unwanted interruption on the way to our desired destination, but it is a passing phase that must not be mistaken for a parking space."

Our failures simply remind us of our humanity. They help us to stay humble and as long as a man is humble, he will be an attraction for God's grace.

Against the background of knowing what failure is not, it is expedient to identify what the various faces of failure look like. Through personal experience and study, I have discovered a number of realities about failure, and different ways in which it manifests.

1. IT IS THE PRICE WE PAY for embracing the spirit of adventure; for daring to become unconventional; for choosing freedom above security. Many times in the pursuit of destiny, we are going to encounter what we call "failure".

2. IT CAN BE THE RESULT OF THE GAP between expectation and actual performance. If there's an expectation placed on a person and

he performs below it, such an outcome could be termed "failure". I have said at different fora that every employee has both an asset value and a replacement value.

Replacement value is determined by the deficit gap between performance on the job and the expectations placed on the performer. It becomes obvious when performance falls below expectation. Economic value on the contrary is revealed when through performance, expectations are exceeded on the job. When we exceed expectations, we have economic value and when we don't, it translates to a replacement value. When an employee tenders his resignation, his boss will either ask "why" or "when", depending on which of the 'values' the employee possesses.

3. IT CAN HAPPEN IF PROCESS IS DISREGARDED or ignored. In life, there are no enduring sudden arrivals; life is all about process. It is process that separates the cosmetic from the authentic. People who have made it to the top will be apt to say that their greatest discovery was not what or where they have attained, but who they became in the process. It is not what a man acquired, but who he became in the process. If in the process of waiting to get a job, you imbibe the right attitude, you would ultimately have become a much better person by the time you get the job.

Any success that lacks history has no future. To everything, there must be a process. I wouldn't give my eleven-year old son the keys to my car yet, not because I don't love him, but actually because I do. I love him too much to destroy him as he does not have the capacity to handle a car yet. He needs to grow, develop and evolve. There are various things we want in life but we do not have the capacity for them yet. So, when we disregard process, we end up failing.

Borrowing wisdom from the scriptures, it can be seen that Saul became king without a process. One day he was anointed, the next day he began ruling. He failed woefully. David was anointed king but it took him thirteen years to come into kingship. Joseph had a dream, but it took over twenty years to see his brothers bow to him. He got to the throne 13 years after his dream, and his brothers did not show up in Egypt until the seven years of abundance were over.

4. AN INCREASE IN RESPONSIBILITY PORTFOLIO without a corresponding increase in capacity will most likely result in failure. There was a time I used to pray for platforms to speak, I would ask God to just open the doors a little and leave me to push the rest open. Even when called to pray at birthday parties, I would seize the opportunity to speak. But presently, my schedule has so much grown that at times, I am called to speak at four places in three

different cities in just one day! My responsibilities have obviously increased. If my capacity for effectiveness does not match the requirements of that portfolio, I will end up becoming a compromise of my brand.

Matching up with the responsibilities often demands making sacrifices and compromising some measure of comfort. This does not translate to living an unbalanced life, but when we understand the seasons of our lives and their demands, we will learn to suspend some things to get the job done.

Everything in life has an explanation; including success and failure. The explanations for success are called "principles" while that of failure are called "excuses". Failure plus excuse do not equate to success. Instead of giving excuses, we should work towards overcoming our challenges and succeeding at all cost.

5. FAILURE CAN BE AS A RESULT OF DISPROPORTIONATE SUCCESS GROWTH. Success sure has several ramifications. I once mentioned that success is when you have peace with God, happiness with yourself, the love of friends and family, and the respect of your enemies. Achieving success at the expense of other vital relationships is a disproportionate success.

Success has to be balanced.

6. FAILURE CAN BE AS A RESULT OF UNFORESEEN CONTINGENCIES. These are things beyond our control. For example, a new government policy can set a hitherto flourishing business back.

7. IT IS A PART OF THE LEARNING PROCESS. This explains why after several failed attempts at his invention, Thomas Edison declared he did not fail, but simply learnt how many ways it wouldn't work. An achiever believes that sometimes we win, and at other times we learn, but we never really lose.

People fail in their careers, businesses, or relationships and it could be at any time. Some fail when they start, others fail mid-way and some fail when they reach the top. We often times wonder why, but our failures simply remind us of our humanity.

They help us to stay humble and as long as a man is humble, he will be an attraction for God's grace.

The things that bring people down from the top are things that follow them there. They are things that have been there all along, but they never took care of them. Nobody starts out to fail in life; it is the accumulation of errors and the repetition of mistakes that culminate in failure.

A Brief Thought on Marital Failures

We have seen several failures in marriages, and it is a trend that still sadly continues. When people exchange their wedding vows, they say "...till death do us part." In my meditation, I have found out that what leads to the failure of marriages is ultimately "death," even when both partners are still living. Marriages fail at the death of interest, affection, and commitment.

These things die gradually without the partners knowing. The "death" begins when issues are left unresolved.

chapter four

MAKING A COMEBACK AFTER A SETBACK

chapter four
MAKING A COMEBACK AFTER A SETBACK

"A man that stops moving will eventually be mourned!"

We must never mistake progress for arrival or take failure as final. Life can only be sustained through progress. A man that stops moving, will eventually be mourned. The best is yet to come, keep at it until you are on top of it.

It was Robert Schuller who wrote a popular book titled "Success is never ending and failure is never final." That is an apt description of the realities of success and failure in life.

The story was said of a woman, whose writings were condemned by her University Professor. Rather than sink into the pool of discouragement and defeat, she kept at what she enjoyed doing and eventually wrote 15 books, which became best sellers. She also became one of the most influential women in America and made multiple appearances on the front cover of Time Magazine. She got over fifteen honorary degrees courtesy of her writing. She became an international celebrity for writing.

Her newspaper column became so syndicated that several other newspapers engaged her as a columnist. That was the same woman who was told by a Professor that if she dared to pursue a career in writing, she would be pursuing a career in crisis. Obviously, the experts are not always right. The negative opinions of other men do not have to become realities in our lives.

One of the best books in my library is a book authored by a man who at one time had wined and dined with the presidents of nations. He actually once owned a whole city in the United States! In the city were two 5 star hotels, each having up to 500 rooms.

He had a state-of-the-art studio; a convertible auditorium that could be turned from a 5,000-seater to a 30-seater including all types of works of art. In one day, he lost everything – all were auctioned!

This was a highly celebrated minister that became bankrupt and eventually was jailed in 1989 on fraud and conspiracy counts. While he was in jail, his wife filed for divorce and later married one of his friends. One moment, he was on top; and the next, he lost it all. It is good to read about people like that to know the pitfalls and how to avoid them and also to know how to make a come-back after a setback. This is necessary because, one way or the other, everyone fails. Of course, no one likes to hear that, but failure is a bus-stop on the way to success. It is the price we have to pay for being adventurous – for daring to leave our comfort zones.

A just man falls seven times and even in the process, he is still called "just". Seven in this context does not refer to the number of times he failed, but the quality of the failure – seven is the number of perfection. The just man fails "perfectly" and one would think there's no hope of a comeback for him. But then, God steps in as his shield and his glory because it's never over until God says it is. No matter what a man has lost, God can restore the years.

Let me also mention the story of the man called Peter J. Daniels. He is a study-in-process for me, as I have chosen to study his life more thoroughly since 2009. Peter J. Daniels is an Australian with a very unfortunate upbringing. He grew up knowing four men to be his father and two women as his mother. A number of his family members went to jail at different times.

At the age of 26, he had no formal education. Today, his family owns a gold and silver bullion bank. That's the same man, who at 26 had no formal education and had failed at virtually everything. His family members lived on welfare, but he rose up to confirm that success is not genetic; neither is failure hereditary, and that a man's background has no right to keep his back on the ground.

Peter J. Daniels has proved a point that no matter how bad your past might have been, your future can be a compensation for it. If you have failed, you are not alone. Someone said, "God is constrained to use failures because there are no other kinds of people except those who have failed!" Looking at the execution of God's agenda for humanity, things appeared at some point to have failed. The bible says after God had made the heavens and the earth, the earth was null and void. God did not make it that way; it became so. Between the first and second verses of Genesis chapter one, there had been an interruption.

Whatever the devil does is never final!

God had an agenda that was unfolding, but there was an interruption to His plan. God however established the fact that whatever the devil does is never final. After the interruption, God began to speak. People may have spoken wrong things into your life, and you kept quiet. You must learn to speak as well. If they say you will not amount to much, say "watch me get there!" No matter what they have said, they will see you arrive at the world of your dreams. The just does not live on the faith of others; he lives by his own faith. If men don't believe in our dreams, we have Joseph as a motivation. They despised him and his dreams, but he kept dreaming.

No matter what your present situation is, just keep on dreaming. They took Joseph's coat of many colours, but they could not take his real attraction – the ability to dream. He dreamt in the pit, and in slavery. Eventually, his dreams came to pass in the palace.

As a student, I used to go for lectures on commercial motorcycles, but in my mind's eyes, I could see myself flying business class in the finest airplanes. Borrow the wings of imagination and see yourself in a preferred future. The future we cannot picture is one we cannot capture. When you cannot picture yourself in that future, you sure cannot feature in it. You have to see it before it becomes a reality.

Steps to handling failure and staging a comeback

1. Once there is a negative occurrence, we must learn to admit that something is wrong. Denial does not delete reality; it only distorts perception. If your car's indicators are telling you there's a problem with the car, it will be foolish to disconnect the indicator and think all is well since there are no more indicators. When things are going wrong, never bandage the damage; treat it.

2. Do an action audit. Ask yourself questions: "what went wrong?", "when did it start?" Never be scared to ask such questions. People usually shy away from such because they don't like to accept responsibility. Asking questions is part of the recovery therapy and the healing process.

3. Learn to forgive. Forgive others and yourself. When things have gone sour, it is expedient to forgive. Forgiveness not only releases the offender; it also releases the offended from becoming a prisoner to the past. The sin you retain will eventually get you detained. Those who allow condemnation enter into depression, but when we allow forgiveness, we are giving ourselves the opportunity to begin again more intelligently. When forgiveness is released, healing begins.

In the 19th century, there was a man named George Wilson in the U.S. On a two-count charge of murder and stealing, he was sentenced to death. However, yielding to the pressure of human rights activists, the President, Andrew Jackson decided to grant him pardon based on the exercise of his prerogative of mercy. To the President's utter dismay and consternation, George Wilson refused the pardon.

The President approached the courts to contest the legality of a convict's right to refuse pardon. The then Chief Justice of the United States – John Marshall in his final ruling on the matter said, "A pardon is a piece of paper.

The value of a pardon is determined by the acceptance of the person to whom it is offered." Since George Wilson refused the pardon, he had to die by hanging. George Wilson died, not for the crime he committed, but for his refusal to accept pardon.

Some people will end up in hell, not for the sins they committed, but for their refusal to accept God's pardon. The difference between Judas and Peter is not in the sins they committed, but in their attitudes towards forgiveness. Judas betrayed Him; Peter denied Him. One entered into self-condemnation and killed himself by hanging; the other turned towards mercy, receiving forgiveness and restoration. Two thieves were crucified with Him; one on the right and the other on the left. They both had a similar history, but their future would certainly not be the same. The difference in their eventualities was not a function of what they did but of their acceptance or refusal of the privilege of pardon from the man that was hanged in between them on the cross.

One of the things we should live with every day is an assurance of God's pardon. We must walk through each day, not as one without an offence, but as one whose account has been cleared. We may not be qualified, but we can be justified. That makes all the difference.

4. Learn the lessons. When we learn the lessons from our losses, they eventually become a blessing. Cornflakes was an error that became a product.

5. Move on. It is important to understand that the best of our days are still ahead of us. A man once said to his son "whenever life knocks you down, make sure you land on your back, because if you land on your back, you can look up; and if you can look up, you can get up."

Everyone falls, but the great ones rise again. The scriptures say a just man falls seven times, but the Lord lifts him up. Every time a just man falls, he picks from the ground, something he can use at the top. We don't embalm the past; we cremate it. We learn the lessons and bury the details. No one looks backwards while driving forward.

6. Believe God for better days. God is the most important personality we will ever have in our lives. The first statement in the bible reads: "In the beginning, God created the heavens and the earth..." There are four basic truths in that sentence: the first personality mentioned was 'God'; the first verb was 'create'; the first location was 'heaven'; and the first time frame was 'the beginning'.

To become achievers, all four are critical to our eventual success in life. The most important time in a man's life is the beginning. That is why the righteous can hardly do anything if the foundations are destroyed. There is something about starting well in life.

The most important personality in our lives is God. For every relationship in life, there is always a substitute, but for God, there is no replacement. God can effectively play man - that is why He is called the father of the fatherless; the husband of the widow; and the friend that sticks closer than a brother. But no man can play God. No man is God to the godless. His shoes are too heavy for a man to wear; His chair is too hot for any man to sit on in our lives. When people walk out of our lives, the doors are open for better people to walk in, but if God walks out of our lives, we are practically done for!

Adam and Eve lost a son to murder and the other to God's judgement. The bible said Adam knew his wife again and she had another son named Seth, which means 'substitute'. There is always a 'Plan B' with God. He is not just the God of a second chance; He is God of another chance! He is the God that can restore and redeem wasted years. He is the only one that can repair what is broken in a man's life.

In Joel 2:3, the bible tells of the land ahead of them as being like the Garden of Eden, and behind them like a wilderness. It doesn't matter what has happened in your past, better days are ahead of you. What was not enough shall come to overflow. You may have experienced rejection, but you'll soon be honoured. The stone rejected by the builders will soon become the chief cornerstone.

chapter five

THE POWER OF KNOWLEDGE

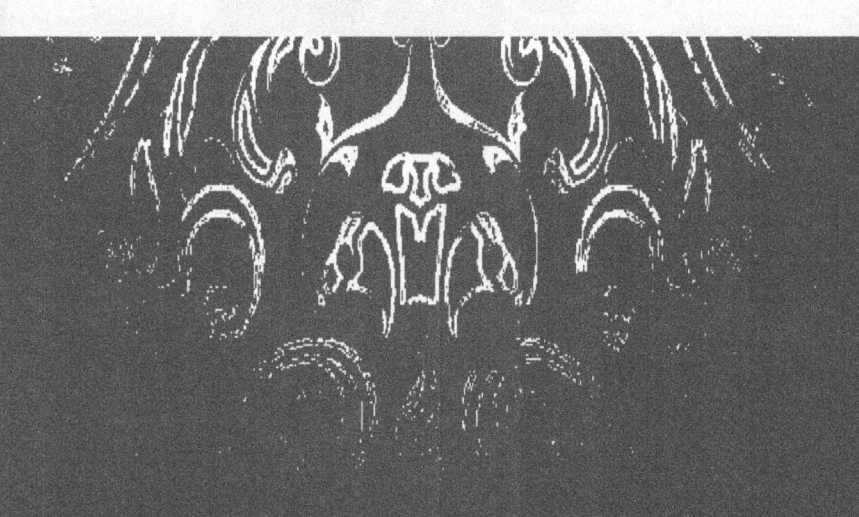

chapter five
THE POWER OF KNOWLEDGE

"You must ensure that your knowledge is fetching you more than your ignorance is costing you."

Knowledge increases your value and self-confidence. Lack of it breeds low self-esteem. There is therefore, wisdom and safety in being a master at something and being sufficiently informed about others.

We will always be indebted to our teachers because what they taught us cannot be returned to them even in moments of anger. No matter how bad the relationship may go, we cannot return the depth of treasure invested in us by our teachers. One of the reasons why armed robbers rarely kill rich people in most developing countries where such crimes are high, is because the survival of the armed robber depends on the continued existence of the rich man! The rich man knows what the robber doesn't. Except for moments of anger and diabolic incursions, robbers rarely kill people because they know what enriched the man is not in his hand, but in his mind. So, even if they take what is in the man's hand, he can always reproduce it.

Never focus on what is in the hand of the rich; find out what is in his mind. When you have the mind of the rich, you will soon have the resources of the rich. It has been discovered that most jackpot winners often return to their old status within ten to twelve months of hitting it. If your money goes up and your mind doesn't, your money will soon return to where your mind is. Your money will definitely shrink to the size of your thinking; it will reduce to the level of your mental capacity.

Lottery is therefore a mockery of the poor by the rich! The rich never became rich through lottery. It is aptly called "jackpot" because it is designed to jack you up and put you back in the pot.

Knowledge is the lightest luggage; yet promises the highest returns. You pay for what you don't know and life pays you for what you know.

The story has been said severally of a man who called a road-side auto repair technician to fix his car after failed attempts at starting the engine. The technician picked up a pebble, gave the battery terminals a couple of knocks and asked the man to start the engine. The car roared back to life. For this seemingly trivial service, the technician billed the car owner fifty dollars ($50), and gave the break-down as $10 for knocking; and $40 for knowing what to knock! When you know what to knock in life, life pays you. But when you don't know what to knock, you pay back.

No man knows it all in life because omniscience is the exclusive preserve of the Almighty God. He has both shared and exclusive attributes. His shared attributes are found in every one of us, but not the exclusive attributes. These are attributes that differentiate Him from men. One of His exclusive attributes is that He is omniscient. It thus becomes a challenge that we can't know everything, considering the fact that we have to pay for what we don't know. It therefore behoves us to make sure that our knowledge can fetch us much more than our ignorance will cost us. Ignorance exerts a force of gravity on all its victims, putting men in a perpetual state of defeat. It is knowledge that frees you from the grounding and limiting effect of ignorance.

Benefits of Apprenticeship

The larger an organisation is, the easier it is for the organisation to take charge of individual errors. Some organisations have systems that "mop up" errors and indemnify the cost implications. There are people who have died in reputable teaching hospitals because of the errors of doctors. No one blames the doctors, but the hospitals. If such doctors however set up their own clinics and people die due to negligence, the doctors would soon be out of jobs. Their errors can be concealed by the bureaucracy in larger organisations.

When you are an apprentice in an organisation, it is essential to learn the secrets of the trade, since every industry has its secret. What gives you an edge over the uninformed stays within your grasp. Men rarely hand such over because it's their critical success factor. Coca-Cola, for example, has a critical success factor that other players in their industry have not been able to master. Working in an organisation therefore gives you access to the secrets of the trade.

"When you don't have a mentor, you'll have to battle your tormentors by yourself."

Working in an organisation also gives you mileage; it places you at an appreciable distance ahead of self-starters.

A man who has pastored a mega church under a thriving ministry will not necessarily go through the typical challenge of beginners when he is called to pioneer his own work. You don't need to have scars to become a star. When you don't have a mentor, you will have to battle your tormentors by yourself.

There is a popular story of a young lawyer who was having problems having an in-road in his career. He was fortunate to be invited for lunch by a more established and successful older lawyer. Expecting to get briefs or referrals from the older lawyer, he was disappointed when after lunch, the older lawyer simply walked him down the street to his office. When people saw him walking with the older lawyer, they concluded he must be worth his salt to merit that relationship. They also reasoned that his services wouldn't be as expensive as that of the older lawyer.

What the young lawyer did not know was that the older lawyer was giving him leverage by walking through the street with him. His career took a new turn after that walk, as he began to get business contacts and opportunities.

If you don't have the privilege of apprenticeship, it is either you don't have a job, or you haven't been a student enough in your posture or attitude to attract a mentor because once the student is ready, the teacher will show up. I go everywhere with the student in me. It is not everywhere I go that the teacher in me finds a door, but there is no place you will ever go without seeing a door for the student in you. Everyone I meet is my potential teacher; I learn from everybody and place a high premium on knowledge.

chapter six

ACCELERATE YOUR SUCCESS RATE

chapter six

ACCELERATE YOUR SUCCESS RATE

"Success is reachable, but not without effort!"

In your journey to your preferred future, you may start small, but aim high, think big and keep moving...fast!

One of the things that determine our net worth and productive value is information or better put - knowledge. My library used to be a bookshelf, but it has outgrown an entire room. Someday, it will be a whole building. It is always a delight having so much wealth of information to draw from. Several books have been written on the subjects of success and failure. It makes sense to have books on failure for two reasons: so as to know the pitfalls and loopholes and how to avoid them. Also in the case of failure, we can know how to make a come-back after a setback.

Success is reachable. This simply means that success will be placed within our reach but not necessarily in our hands. If we can reach out, we can reach it. Riches are not limited to the reach of the rich. They are within the reach of anyone who will reach out for them. In the days of racial segregation in the U.S, Mrs. S. B. Fuller said to her 7 year-old son, "We are not poor because of God; neither are we poor because of our skin color. Black is not synonymous with lack." It has been rightly said that a man's background should not keep his back on the ground. The woman said to her son, "We are poor because your daddy has never desired to be rich". People become rich because they desire to be rich, while some others are poor because they have never desired to be anything else. 'Que sera sera', whatever will be will be. Unfortunately, good things don't come like that; you have to go out for them. Whatever a man cannot do is what he has not attempted to do. If you will dare it, you will do it.

What does it mean to accelerate your success rate?

It means to increase your momentum. To accelerate means to speed up, increase or hasten the power or rate of movement. Acceleration demands taking personal responsibility. Nobody should be as interested in your success as yourself. You have to assume the driver's seat as far as your life is concerned. You have to take your life in your hands.

There are basically four reasons why we have to step up or accelerate in life:

1. We were designed for movement.

Every individual made by God was designed for movement. Naturally by design, we exhibit an irritation to stagnation. Success is progressive. No matter how well we are doing, we often come to a point where we are dissatisfied with our performance. Where you are today may be someone else's dream, but you have conquered that point. People may not understand why you are not happy, but the truth is that you are seeing something bigger and better than where you are now.

When a man progresses in life, he goes beyond asking God for daily bread, to demanding for a higher level of significance. He does not just cry to God to meet his needs because they have increased. His needs would have become the needs of more families because he has to pay the salaries of their breadwinners. Looking at our lives in retrospect, we would realise that where we are today was a dream five years ago. Today, it has become a reality and the excitement of the initial attainment is fast waning.

2. Everything that is living is moving, including the clock.

You can only stop your watch, but you cannot stop Time. Everything living is moving. One of the signs of death is lack of movement. So anyone who does not move will soon be mourned.

3. There is no status quo ante.

Everything in the realm of time is subject to change. The only things that don't change are things beyond the boundary of time. That is why God can say, "I am the Lord, I change not," because even though He works in time, He lives outside of it. Time was given, not just to prepare man for eternity, but also to protect man from it. Everything within the confines of time is subject to change. "No condition is permanent" is the language of time. There are universities that were once reputed to be good universities, but all they have today are just names.

In the sixties, it was said that the University College Hospital, in southwestern Nigeria was the fourth best hospital in the Commonwealth. Unfortunately, the story is very different today with the slide on the reverse. Over time, things have changed.

4. The challenge of the future.

There is always something about the future. It has the capacity to make what is small today to be big, and what is big today to be small tomorrow. We should all be interested in the future because that is where we will spend the rest of our lives. Today was the future you spoke about yesterday. The future is a place in time that is longer than today. It is the opportunity of a loser to become a winner; the chance for the failure to begin again more intelligently. It is the permission of the poor to become rich. It is also the challenge of the rich to stay rich or become richer.

There used to be a popular saying among the residents of Ibadan in Nigeria. They would say, "O ko'le bi ile Adebisi" (he built a house like Adebisi's). It got me wondering what was special about Adebisi's house. It derived its reputation from either being the first storey building in Ibadan or perhaps the most magnificent in its time. To satisfy my curiosity, I decided to go see the so-called edifice. When I was taken there, I had to ask "where is the house?" It is obviously a house whose grandeur has lost relevance over time. I would rather call it an historical monument. But it used to be the pride of the city. By virtue of the power of the future, it is no longer the edifice it used to be. It used to be "the building" but today, it is merely a relic.

There are people who could not afford a bag of cement when it was sold for just five cents, but the same people are building mansions now that a bag of cement costs about ten dollars. People who could not build houses before have turned what used to be castles into chalets, courtesy of the power of the future.

"The future is so powerful and it is usually filled with surprises."

When Martin Luther (the reformer) was in high school, he had a teacher who would bow to his students before starting his class. The man had his reason. He was not bowing to who they were, but to who they would become. He was bowing to their future.

A woman once put a baby in a basket and asked her daughter to watch over it. Little did the girl know that the baby in the basket was the key to her deliverance from captivity. The baby in the basket was Moses and the setting was Egypt; the stage was the River Nile and the sister was Miriam. If she did not take care of the baby, she would have to live up to her name, which meant bitterness. The future is so powerful and it is usually filled with surprises! So, because of the challenge of the future, we have to speed up, accelerate and move fast. How do we achieve that?

Think Long Term

Learn to plan as much as 20 years ahead. It has been discovered that those who do well in the moment are those who do not just live for the moment. Organisations that do well are those that plan with a long term perspective, same goes for individuals that do well. The reason we have savings is because we think about the future. We are so sure the future will come. There is a movie called "If tomorrow comes." I would rather say "when tomorrow comes" because tomorrow will come, it is just a matter of time.

Ben Carson counsels that as we live our lives every day, we should ask ourselves what we will have to do in twenty years down the line. He says if that is not enough of a motivation, we could ask the question "what will I not like to be doing twenty years from now?" The future is never a gift but a result; it is not an accident but a consequence. It is a result of our actions and inactions today.

New 'hires' of a Nigerian bank were said to have been taken on a visit to the Kirikiri prison in Lagos as part of their orientation exercise. They were taken there to see those who used to matter in banking, but have ended up in jail. After the visit to the jail, they proceeded to the house of the bank's chairman somewhere on the Lagos Island - a beautiful waterfront mansion. That was meant to show them the other side of the coin. That one-day experience stayed with them longer than all they had been taught in one month.

We should occasionally visit the prisons. It will help us curb our excesses. There are always boundaries in life. Cars are made with brakes. A car without a brake is a potential casket. If you don't learn how to set the limits for yourself, the society will set them for you.

Children must be taught to know there are boundaries. There are a lot of adults today, who are dysfunctional in their adulthood, because when they were growing up, their parents never established boundaries for them.

Some individuals in prisons ended up there because they abused their freedom when they had it. Learn to think long term. Picture the kind of parent you would want to be. Upon my return from a foreign trip, my 6 year-old son saw my luggage, and said to me
"Daddy, you are a successful man."
When he said that, I made up my mind that I had to live up to it.

"There are always boundaries in life."

Conditions for Success

Success occurs when the grace of God is appropriated by the efforts of man. However, there are certain conditions which largely rest on human discipline.

1. Pay the price because everything has a price. Every dream has an altar, and every altar demands sacrifice. A dreamer gives up to go up. Nothing is free, not even in Freetown. If they called it free, someone must have paid for it. There are toll gate requirements for moving up in life.

2. Mind the company you keep. Where you belong has a direct influence on who you become. A man cannot walk with giants, eat what they eat and remain small. Everybody has an atmosphere – some, a fragrance; others an odour. Over time, you will begin to smell like the company you keep. If they have a fragrance, you will soon smell like them, and if they have an odour, they will certainly spread it to you. Friendship is by choice, not by force. It is a gift; not a right. When you give access to a person, you have given him the right to influence you either positively or negatively. Mind your company because access breeds influence. It has been proven that most successful people rarely have more than five to seven strong relationships in their lives. I have acquaintances and associates, but friendship is a deep word; it comes with a lot of commitment.

3. Evaluate. Do a stock-taking; take an inventory; measure your progress. Organisations often do this periodically. You ought to constantly evaluate yourself to know if you are making progress. Waiting for a year to do this may be too long. The biblical standard is daily – "Teach us to number our days..."[1] If a day does not add up, a year cannot. Life is an accumulation of moments. Success is making measurable progress in a reasonable amount of time. There is an appropriate fruit for every stage of a man's life. If at 50, you have a

testimony that you should have had at 35, it is no longer a testimony. That is why the bible says, "Satisfy us early with your mercy…"

4. Shoot your cannon balls up. I once heard this from someone and it blessed me. The story was said of how the Germans had tried to invade Russia during the Second World War. There was a mass of water that was meant to serve as access for the Germans. At that period of the year, the water surface had largely turned into solid ice and the Germans were hoping to take advantage of that to ride into Russia. After several attempts at defrosting the ice, someone on the Russian side came up with the idea of firing cannon balls into the air just above the water, such that the balls would hit the ice surface with so much force, thus breaking it up. They took that option and it did the magic.

The morale of the story is that by shooting the cannon balls up, their efforts gained momentum, and became successful. Shooting the cannon balls up speaks of getting God involved in the affairs of our lives. "Except the Lord builds a house, they labour in vain that build it." 2 The key that opens the door no man can shut is the key of David. People succeed not just because they are intelligent, but because they were assisted. The battle is not to the strong but to the strengthened. Paul may plant and Apollos may water but it is God that gives the increase.

Some people may be your age mates or class mates but they are not necessarily your "grace mates." Grace is making progress at heaven's expense. It is synonymous to a mother carrying a baby on her back. When the mother climbs up, the baby automatically moves up as well. The baby is going up without climbing because the effort of upward mobility rests on the one carrying the baby. There are usually two ways of going up a skyscraper – through the staircase or by using the elevator. With the staircase, you may make it to the top, but not at the same time as the person who uses the elevator, and not in the same condition.

Some people jump up. When you jump up, you will come down. Jumping up makes you touch the ceiling faster, but you will still come down. This is a metaphor for looking blessed without being truly blessed. Many people act IT but they are not really IT. Then there are those who climb up, but being lifted up is a better realm. There are hands that lift up – they are the hands of God. The Bible said of Uzziah that for as long as he sought the Lord, God made him to prosper.

"The key that opens the door no man can shut is the Key of David."

It is possible to attract with ease what others struggle and strive to attain. For example, a good wife is simply an inheritance from the Lord (Prov 19:14).

Because our understanding is limited, our human vulnerability makes us liable to poor choices without God's help.

May I implore you at this point to take out a few minutes to shoot cannon balls? I'm sure there are grounds you desire to break in different aspects of your life. You don't have to pray long, just pray right!

chapter seven

STAYING ON TOP

chapter seven
STAYING ON TOP

"You can decide to be envied rather than be pitied."

In the pursuit of success, many people have become important to others but strangers to themselves. The children they once were are not proud of the adults they have become.

In 1999, after leaving banking, I returned to the city where I grew up in pursuit of purpose and decided to empty my account to purchase electronics for my new apartment. Before going to get the electronics, I branched at a bookshop, and seeing the books on display, I had a change of mind. I told myself that in 10 years time, nobody would reward me for being a disc jockey; I'd rather be rewarded for being the best in what I've been called to do; being an apex personality in my chosen field. So I emptied my purse into that bookshop.

Mark Twain said, "When you empty your purse into your head, the returns will be more than what your purse can contain." I once was invited to a TV interview where we were talking about the value of knowledge. I went with about twenty books from my library. One of the interviewers looked at the books and asked if they were available because he had only seen one of them before. I told him they were available. He went ahead to ask if they were affordable. I said "Affordability is a matter of priority." There are people who would rather invest their money in 'aso ebi' (uniform attires for social occasions), but I chose to empty my resources into the purchase of books. Why? A step upward in knowledge is a step forward in life. So, when knowledge is not updated, you become outdated. What do we call redundancy? It is when an environment has outgrown your relevance.

It is a man's capacity for achievement that determines his rewards in life. In life, we are paid in direct proportion to what we do, how well we do it and how easy or difficult it is to find a replacement for us.

What determines your economic value to an organisation is the measure of their expectation as regards your performance vis-à-vis your ability to exceed that expectation. That is, when you are given a job to do and you exceed expectations, you have a high economic value and are not easily disposable; but when you perform below expectations, you obviously have a huge replacement value.

People say there are no jobs but that is false because, every day, job opportunities are advertised. But every job has certain qualifications attached to it.

So, your ability to develop capacity for the expectation of the market place, determines how much of indispensability you will possess.

Gravity is a natural phenomenon. Everything is in a natural state of decline. Every product has an expiry date. From the moment it is produced, the countdown towards expiration begins. So it is with men. You may not agree, but human beings also have expiry dates. Some folks can no longer do the things they used to do five years ago, because their life is moving towards expiration gradually. No matter how much faith a man can exercise, there will come a time when wrinkles will begin to appear. Those are signs of ageing. Ageing is natural; development is not. Since gravity is also a natural phenomenon, one of the things organisations and some individuals do is to develop an intervention process, which is aimed at halting the process of decline.

> "Gravity is a natural phenomenon, but up thrust is a deliberate initiative."

Intervention processes are engineered to halt the process of decline, which is a natural process.

For machines, the intervention process is called 'maintenance', but for humans, it is called 'training'. Gravity is a natural phenomenon, but upthrust is a deliberate initiative. What does it take to come down? Simply do nothing to stay up. Nobody falls up; they climb up. People fall down, but they don't fall up. When you see someone doing well, you may not be able to explain his results, but certain forces must have gone into play for him to achieve those results. Some years ago, I asked someone what was the secret of his success. He said it was the grace of God. I begged to differ because the bible says the grace of God has appeared to all men.

Why do some look 'graced' and others disgraced? You will recall that in high school mathematics, the outcome of an equation is not determined by the constant, but by the variables. The grace of God is the constant in life's equation. It is therefore not the sole determinant of a man's outcome. There is a variable called 'self-help' or 'individual effort'. It is the ability not to take the grace of God in vain; assuming responsibility for our eventualities. Whether you succeed or fail, the person most responsible for the outcome is the one whose face you see each time you look into the mirror.

A set of twins were given birth to by an alcoholic father, who was a nuisance to the neighbourhood. He did not amount to much. As the twins grew, one of them turned out exactly like the father – a complete failure. On the contrary, the other one became very successful, unlike the father. At separate interviews, they were both asked about the reason for their outcomes in life. The unsuccessful twin said "I had no choice; I had to become like my father."

> "The grace of God is the constant in life's equation. It is therefore not the sole determinant of a man's outcome."

The other twin was asked why he did not turn out like his father. He replied "I had no choice but to succeed. My father was a failure and I did not want my past to repeat itself in my future." No matter what your past might have looked like, your future can be a compensation for it. Even though we are the offspring of the past, we are also parents of the future. You have the power to take responsibility for your eventualities. A man can decide in life to be pitied or envied.

Good Success

There is a big difference between success and "good success." Good success is light years ahead of success. Success is getting what you want, while good success is wanting what you got after getting it! Good success has four components:
1. Peace with God.
2. Happiness with yourself.

3. Experiencing the love and admiration of your friends and family.
4. Earning the respect of your enemies.

These four are non-negotiable components of good success. There are people who sweat in air-conditioned rooms because there is no peace in their heart. A bank employee was said to have made away with over a hundred thousand dollars belonging to the bank.

No matter how far he runs, his conscience will still haunt him. He can't run away from himself. There are people who buy sleeping pills but still can't sleep.

Money can buy sleeping pills but not sleep. The book I proffer as the manual for success, teaches me that it is God who gives sleep to His beloved. So, peace with God is very essential.

> **"Work without love results in a fractured life."**

Many people in pursuit of success become important to others but strangers to themselves. The children they once were are no longer proud of the adults they have become. There also has to be the love of friends and family because life is basically about working and loving. Work without love results in a fractured life. Robert Schuller told the story of a man who had just three people at his burial, though he was survived by a wife and three grown-up sons. He was a multi-millionaire in dollars before he died. He was buried in the same city where his wife and three sons resided, but only three people were present at his burial – the person that brought the body from the mortuary, the preacher that committed the body to the earth, and the body itself! He achieved success at the expense of his family. That is certainly not good success.

"At the heart of man's existence is the desire to be intimate and loved by someone else. Life's deepest meanings are not found in accomplishments but in relationships."

chapter eight

THE CHALLENGE OF SUCCESS SUSTAINABILITY

chapter eight
THE CHALLENGE OF SUCCESS SUSTAINABILITY

"It takes work to go up, but more work to stay up. Indolence can never sustain the rewards of diligence."

The rays of light have no respect for age. Therefore, in life there are no age mates, only illumination colleagues because age mates are not always mates and classmates do not always end up in the same class.

There are usually two types of players in every industry – the leader labels and the play-alongs. It has been observed that 90% of trade in any industry is controlled by 15% of the participants in the industry. Those players are called the "leader labels". The play-alongs usually exist to make up the numbers.

In life, you either pick a jersey or buy tickets. It is easier to buy a ticket than to get a jersey. Getting a jersey requires a greater measure of training and discipline. I have also observed that there are certain people who have jerseys but do not differ much from those who bought tickets. Such people only run the length of the field without making an impact.

A footballer asking for the ball for 90 minutes is definitely not relevant; he is simply a mobile spectator. All he has is the privilege of presence and not the evidence of impact!

There are people who merely make up the numbers in their industries. Their inferiority and non-performance establishes the superiority of the leader labels, because superiority needs inferiority to exist. The position of the leader label is however not invincible. That a man is doing well does not mean he will always do well. It takes work to go up, but more work to stay up. Indolence and indulgence cannot maintain the result of diligence. We have seen mega conglomerates become corporate catastrophes!

There are basically two things responsible for the loss of market leadership:

1. The presence of 'competing competitors'

Not all competitors are spectators. There are silent players in some industries who are actually not sleeping. While at school, it was so easy to identify the competition. You met them in class; at the library; and virtually everywhere on the campus. You therefore had an idea of how they were preparing and could easily match up with them. However, outside of school, it's an open field. There is no fence around the world, neither is there a ceiling over it.

> **"Money always flows from the watchers to the performers!"**

Movie producers rarely have time to watch what they produce by the time it is premiered. While people are flocking the theaters, they are busy producing more to keep us watching. Money always flows from the watchers to the performers! So we pay them for entertaining us. Being oblivious of the competition's preparation may undermine your effort at performance. You will never know how badly you are doing until pay day comes. Every competition comes with more than a prize. However, there will always be just one prize for the winner. That is the prize. Others are consolation prizes.

The sleeplessness of your competition may soon turn to nightmares for you. Henry Ford said "Everybody works when it is work time... it is the so-called leisure time that colleagues use to get ahead of their contemporaries." Age mates are not always mates and classmates do not always end up in the same class. In life there are no age mates; only illumination colleagues. In the National Assembly, there are thirty five year-old legislators and sixty year-old legislators; they are colleagues and will address each other as such! Age thus becomes just a number. The position one person got to at sixty was attained by another at thirty-five. The rays of light have no respect for age. The time will always come when respect becomes mere courtesy because the real measure of respect is result. Without results, there may be plenty of insults.

The presence of a competitor breaks the monopoly of the "gurus" and gives consumers the privilege of options in any market. The competition is made up of people who are constantly thinking of how they can outperform, 'out-think', and 'out-produce' the industry leaders. It may take years but the agenda of the market-place insurgents is to unseat the incumbents.

"Every competition comes with more than a prize- Winner prize and Consolation prizes. Choose!"

2. The customer is a moving target

It used to be said that the consumer is king. That would have been true a century ago, when royalty commanded greater authority. Today, royalty is largely a ceremonial status. The customer is therefore more than a king; he is sovereign. The customer keeps every business running. Employees may leave and the business continues, but the moment the customers leave, the business dies.

A young man was telling his grand-father that he had started business. He said, "We have set up the office, printed our business cards, and started the television adverts..." The grandfather simply asked "what about patronage?" The law of the market-place demands that the seller shows up before the buyer. Business however doesn't start until the buyer shows up.

The customer is a democrat who votes with his feet and he doesn't wait for four years to exercise his electoral powers; he votes as often as he wishes. The customer is a moving target and your greatest sales influence. He can be won or lost. Bear in mind that in business, your greatest success is usually tied to the recommendation of others. Although Joseph could interpret dreams, someone had to recommend him to Pharaoh. David could play the harp, but someone had to mention his name to Saul. It is therefore implied that if you don't enjoy recommendations, you are likely to struggle before you eventually emerge.

Sustaining Marketplace Leadership

Irrespective of the nature of the business, there are basically two things that will help sustain success and marketplace leadership: brand value and effective customer relations. These are time-tested principles with predictable outcomes.

Brand Value

The success of any product lies in its consumer appeal. For any product to succeed in the marketplace, it must appeal to the consumer. As earlier stated in this book, where money is not a constraint, and several products offer similar solutions, brand preference is determined by value. That value can be real or imagined, but nonetheless, it is value. Value largely depends on who defines it. Many organisations erroneously define value inside out. Value must be defined outside in. It is the consumer, and not the producer that places value on a product. To the staff of a company, value is customer service, but to the consumer, value is customer satisfaction. To the staff, value is product-driven, but to a consumer, value is experience driven.

When a customer goes into an eatery, he expects to also get some courteous welcome, and the ambience of a beautiful atmosphere. According to Peter Drucker, we are living in the era of the 3Cs: tremendous competition, accelerated change, and overwhelming complexity. When a customer comes to a place, he enters with an expectation, but he leaves with an experience. He can come in curious but leaves with an opinion.

At first contact, a consumer may relate with the name of your brand, but after the first contact, he begins to relate with the experience he has had. When customer expectation exceeds customer experience, a customer has been lost potentially. But when customer experience exceeds customer expectation, then potentially, a customer has been won.

Businesses commonly say "If we please you, tell others, if we don't tell us." Unfortunately, if you please the customer, he will tell others and if you don't, he will also tell others; not you. Everybody has a circle of influence and usually, when you lose one person, you are most likely losing everybody within his or her circle of influence. The potential of a customer can therefore not be under-estimated; either won or lost. People most often meet the product before the producer. A product is the producer's signature. The Latin word for a work of art is the same word for 'character', which implies that a man's work is his lengthened shadow.

Effective Customer Relations

When it comes to effective customer relations, it is necessary to understand the four postures customers typically have towards any product: suspects, prospects, clients, and loyalists. There are people who form their opinions about a product from a distance. We call them suspects. They become cynical without giving the product the privilege to prove its claim. The job of every good salesman is to be able to move anybody from the level of a suspect to that of a loyalist.

A prospect on the other hand fantasizes about a product even though he hasn't had any contact with it. Eventually, he becomes a client and begins to patronize the product. There are defining moments for any product. A good example is when a prospect decides to be a client. Such moments don't come announced. We therefore do not get ready; we live ready. Based on whatever relationship developed between that person and the product or the producer, he may likely become a loyalist. A loyalist is not just a patron; he feels a sense of co-ownership of the product. With time, he begins to tell others about it. It is said that the highest level of marketing is not direct marketing but indirect marketing. That is when customers become advocates of the product.

Know your Customer

Assumption is said to be the lowest level of intelligence. Many people merely assume their position in the market place without knowledge of the customer and his opinion. Entering into the Nigerian market, a foreign producer of dairy products studied the market and realised there were leader labels in the industry. The leader labels had carved niches for themselves. This new entrant decided to package powdered milk in small sachets in order to make them affordable for people who had thought that milk was beyond their reach. They therefore made the mass-market their focus, and interestingly, that market segment was more populated than the top-of-the-pyramid people who could afford tinned milk. Rather than compete in the existing terrain, they carved out another niche. They identified a customer segment and knew what suited them. Other milk producers have followed their model; even the leader labels.

"Assumption is said to be the lowest level of intelligence."

that market segment was more populated than the top-of-the-pyramid people who could afford tinned milk. Rather than compete in the existing terrain, they carved out another niche. They identified a customer segment and knew what suited them. Other milk producers have followed their model; even the leader labels.

Knowing your customer requires the development of a feedback mechanism. It is however not just enough to collect feedback; acting on the results is very critical. Many organisations collect feedbacks but never act on them. The feedbacks help businesses feel the pulse of their customers and know their peculiar needs. If you don't take care of a customer, somebody is waiting eagerly to relieve you of the burden of relevance.

Train Your Personnel

Continuous training and motivation of staff, especially front-desk officers are very essential to any business that must survive in today's competitive environment. Front-desk staff members are the interface between the organization and the customers. Whatever impression they create for the customer becomes the image the customer has of the entire organization. I have observed that in every organization, there are two GMs and they are equally powerful. The General Manager and the Gate Man!

"If you think education is expensive, try ignorance."

The story was told of a man who went to a bank after closing hours and was rudely denied access by the security man. The security man may have been right about the closing time, but his service delivery left more to be desired. The customer turned back and closed his account the next day. He was a customer worth five million dollars! The bank lost a key customer, not to the impoliteness of the security man, but to their non-investment in the security man's training. Every time you think of the cost of training, consider the cost of not training. The only thing worse than losing employees is keeping them without training them. Like the saying goes "if you think education is expensive, why not try ignorance?"

Tell them what they need to know and don't stop telling them because knowledge can be slippery in nature. Do it again, and again, and again. It's an overhauling process; it's an intervention process against the force of decline. If you do these things as an organization or an individual, you will keep smiling to the bank!

Creating a Valuable Brand

Before talking about a valuable brand, it is essential to understand what a brand is. A brand can simply be described as a label; an identity badge; a stamp of recognition; your point of exclusivity; your DNA or your thumb-print. Those are things that will not make you have a mistaken identity.

A brand makes your voice stand out in a crowd. Branding helps you choose what you will be remembered for. A lot of consumers make their shopping decisions based on the sentiments they have for particular brands. Your brand distinguishes you from the competition, and gives you an edge. There is a popular brand of food seasoning in Nigeria that has become the defining brand for all other seasonings in the country. I grew up knowing all seasonings by the name of that particular one, and I would always ask for it, even when I meant to ask for another seasoning. A successful brand is the one that lives perpetually in the minds of its consumers and delivers distinctive benefits.

Even in ministry, some people have become brands. When we think of faith, Kenneth Hagin's name readily comes to mind. Billy Graham in the U.S has become a brand of integrity; the brand of honour. Republicans and Democrats become friends at Billy Graham's meetings because he is a father to all. His name has consistently been on the roll of honour for decades now.

I heard about a popular brand of car with so many value-added security features, and excellent after-sales services from the major distributors. There is a customized version of the car, which can seal up itself and generate oxygen for six hours, in the event of an attack. If the tyres are shot, the car could still be driven for a hundred kilometers. Of course, when the car is taken to the service center, the car owner is given a courtesy car to use while his car is under repair. That is no doubt an excellent brand.

"...brand is defined by what people call it."

A brand is built internally within the confines of an assembly plant, but its endorsement comes externally. You may call your product by any name, but the brand is defined by what people call it. The effective management of perception is what adverts are all about. Unfortunately, adverts only promote brands; they don't create brands. Brands are created when:
- Products deliver as promised;
- Products perform consistently without compromise;
- There is an investment in spiritual capital.

For products to deliver as promised, quality control becomes very essential. Beyond the delivery of service promise, consistent performance is also necessary. An eatery recently opened in my neighbourhood, and I decided to patronize it. I ordered for fruit salad, and was surprised to find a metal in it! I couldn't help wondering what fruit had a metal. Could there be 'metallic oranges'? What I actually found was a staple pin! After tasting two staple pins in two spoons of fruit salad, I had to abandon it. I took a bite out of the chicken I bought, and it was stale. I left dissatisfied and queried how old they were in the business to be compromising value. There was no consistency in their performance.

The Spiritual Capital

I have a personal conviction, which was confirmed by some Harvard scholars that companies which will define the business landscape in the future will be those with 'spiritual capital.' In the opinion of the Harvard scholars, having a spiritual capital means doing good. That is the spirit behind corporate social responsibility. Capitalism as it is currently practiced is based on two pre-suppositions:

1. Humans are primarily economic beings who thrive in an environment dominated by money.
2. Humans are selfish beings who will always act rationally to improve their own financial best interest.

The second presupposition has however been faulted fundamentally because it creates a terminal value to any satisfaction derived from our achievement. It ties the limits of personal fulfilment to finances. The craving of the human heart seeks fulfilment that cannot be met by that which is only material and self-seeking. The human heart seeks answers to questions of meaning. Intelligence has been defined as the tool we use to cultivate our lives and to wield control over our environment. There are three types of intelligence: logical, emotional, and spiritual.

Most people are familiar with normal or logical intelligence, which is the basic type of intelligence. There is however a different type of intelligence called 'emotional intelligence.' That is the level of intelligence required in management levels. At such levels, you need less of logical intelligence and more of emotional intelligence, because there are pressures that go with leadership. As a manager, you need more of people skills than job skills.

Beyond emotional intelligence, people also need spiritual intelligence. Spiritual intelligence is the bringing to bear of a God-consciousness; an eternal consciousness and the need for significance in our pursuit of business success. The secular world has therefore discovered that for you to pace yourself effectively, you need intelligence on all three planes.

Daniel found relevance with Darius and Cyrus. That was not just relevance in two political regimes; it was relevance in two different kingdoms. Despite the changes in governance, there was someone whose inputs could not be ignored – Daniel. He prospered in every regime because of his investment in spiritual capital. Job was said to be the richest man in the east, at a time when the east was the richest place on earth.

He was therefore the richest man living. The basis for his riches was the fear of God; his investment in spiritual capital.

The pyramids of Egypt have outlived all the other wonders of the ancient world because they were built on the 'preservation technology' recommended by Joseph to Egypt. That was a technology birthed by spiritual revelation.

My submission therefore is that what will give you and I a competitive advantage in the world will be our walk with God.

> "Spiritual intelligence is the bringing to bear of a God-consciousness."

Some years ago, my wife miraculously got a job she did not even apply for at a telecoms firm. At the interview, she was asked a question on a topic she was taught in her first year at the university. At that point, the board on which her lecturer wrote several years back was brought into her view! That was an obvious result of the spiritual investment we are talking about.

During World War II, there was a surging demand for ocean vessels and earth moving machines. Meeting up with such a demand was a major challenge until a man named R.G Letourneau came into the picture. He was a man who had been denied formal education because he was too dull to read.

Things however changed when he met God and began to serve Him. He had become a mechanic and God poured out creative ideas into his mind. No wonder he became the man with the solution; a best-selling brand in his own right. Investment in spiritual capital sure makes all the difference.

chapter nine

SUCCESSION PLANNING

chapter nine

SUCCESSION PLANNING

"Learn, learn, keep learning and then... take the lead!"

Everybody is a visible expression of the realities they are exposed to. Exposure to learning through mentoring is the process of bringing the leader out of the follower.

Permit me to share a thought with you. Most cars moving commuters on our roads fall into one of three categories: those in traffic, those in a convoy, and those in a competition. When driving, there will always be a category of people behind you, who just happen to have been caught in traffic. They may not necessarily be going in your direction. There are also those who are in your convoy. They turn to wherever you go. And there are those who are possibly in a race with you. For those in traffic, you share no sentiments while with those in your convoy, you share a common destination. However, for those in a race, the basis of your relationship is a competition.

As you move from one location to another in life, be mindful of those three categories of people. A man cannot rise beyond the quality of the influence in his life. We are direct products of the investments of the associations in our lives. Our friends are a prophecy of our future. They could determine the quality of our end.

There are people who are supposed to be in our convoy but get trapped in the "traffic" mind-set. That's because they don't emulate the things we initiate.

Whatever they behold in our lives, they do not have a desire to become in theirs. To make the most of your existence, it is important to discern those who are in traffic and ensure you do not expend your energy in that direction because that will be a waste.

While we must make allowances for slow learners and eventual catchers, our focus in the immediate must be on those who have developed the appetite and posture of an eager learner. In every leading organization, there is something called 'succession planning' which is built into their structures. It is informed by the understanding that the current players in the organization will not be there forever, no matter how good they are. It isn't a matter of 'if tomorrow comes' but 'when tomorrow comes'. We therefore have to establish a succession planning framework that will help recognize those who will take over when the baton has to change hands.

> **"Mentoring is the process of bringing the leader out of the learner."**

The process of identifying and mentoring the 'generation-next' is what we call 'succession planning'. Mentoring is the process of bringing the leader out of the learner. It is the process of bringing the star out of the player; the professional out of the amateur. You cannot bring a leader out of someone who is not a learner. Mentoring can only happen when someone has a meal, and another has an appetite for that meal. A mentor is not someone who craves your respect; he is someone who commands it. He is someone whose instructions you follow. To attempt to mentor someone who is not a learner will only result in 'force-feeding'.

Relationships in our lives will fall into one of these categories: up-line, on-line, or down-line. We need to know who belongs where. It is identity crisis when you behave like a father in a place where you are supposed to be a son. It is equally an identity crisis to behave like a colleague when you are supposed to be a father.

The Genius Within

Everybody is an entrepreneur of some sorts, because we all carry talent, uniqueness, and creativity. Those are the hallmarks of an entrepreneur. Talent is a divine deposit that is not your decision but your discovery. Uniqueness consists of the things that define your exclusivity. Those are the things that differentiate you from others. Some people are so uniquely accustomed to frowning that even when they want to smile, they frown! Lack of humour has become a brand for them.

Everyone is creative. At least, we have all told lies at some point in time. If you deny ever lying, then you have just told another lie! The ability to lie is creativity that lacks appropriate focus. Falsehood is creativity in operation. If you can find appropriate focus for it, it becomes ingenuity. So, everyone has talent, uniqueness and creativity. Everyone is therefore a potential entrepreneur.

> "The emergence of that genius in you requires your active and deliberate participation."

Education is a combination of schooling and apprenticeship. Schooling is the process of refining the entrepreneur, and it happens in a formal institution of learning. Apprenticeship is however the process of reviving the entrepreneur and it commences the moment you get a job. A job is therefore not an end in itself, but a means to an ordained outcome – the awakening of the entrepreneur on your inside.

Some years ago, the 'Human Advancement Technology' was discovered in America. It was borne out of the need to reintegrate World War II veterans to normal life. First, they had to be demilitarized. The aftermath effects of war needed to be dealt with. It is very much similar to colonialism. Apartheid ended in South Africa in 1994, but many South Africans still live with the scars. Apartheid has done so much damage to the psyche of many. There are several men in the townships who spend their earnings on alcohol, while the women run the homes and get better educated.

The scenario is similar to that of the Israelites. They left Egypt physically but still carried Egypt in their minds. The Egyptians died on the seashore, but their effects did not. The human advancement technology is a strategy for the systematic desensitization of a man from a mind-set that is conditioned to failure, and a reprogramming of the man with a new desire to succeed.

There are men who practically have no thirst for success, irrespective of their age. Thank God Abraham was called at 75. At that age, he was still living in his father's house!

The human advancement strategy postulates that everyone was born with a genius. The emergence of that genius is however a process that requires active participation of the individual in question. Frederick Douglas said,

"Our destiny is in our hands. If we must find, we will have to seek. If we are poor, the economic well-being of others will only compound our misery." If out of envy, you decide to pull down someone moving forward, his downfall will not translate to your upward mobility, because his progress is not a reason for your stagnancy.

chapter ten

BUILDING SPIRITUAL CAPITAL

chapter ten
BUILDING SPIRITUAL CAPITAL

"...That thy profiting may appear to all."

Happy are those who reject the advice of evil people, who do not follow the example of sinners or join those who have no use for God...

They are like trees that grow beside a stream, that bear fruit at the right time, and whose leaves do not dry up. They succeed in everything they do.

We established in the last chapter that spiritual capital is doing good and making significant eternal impact. Success should not just be a spiritual experience that nobody can see. Yes, it will start like that, it will start from the invisible, but it must become visible eventually. When you are fruitful, your life will be impactful, generating positive consequence and making a meaning. In other words, your existence is dispensing good to other people. However there are eight timeless principles we need to be reminded of from time to time about living a fruitful life.

1. Be Seed Conscious

Everything was made with the seed of it in it. The only way to perpetuate anything is through the seed. We have been told that we can all count the number of seeds in the apple fruit, but nobody can tell the number of trees in the apple seed, because in every apple seed that is sown, there is a potential for many trees to grow. So you can actually not tell how many trees are in the seed. All you can count is the number of seeds in the fruit. And in every seed, there is the possibility of a forest. Therefore, you have to be seed conscious! God will promise you a harvest, but place a seed in your hand. God will promise you the future, but he will give you today, God will promise you greatness but all that God will give to you will be an opportunity for service. God will promise you long life but he will give you an opportunity to honour people in your life especially your parents.

"The only way to perpetuate anything is through the seed."

As you sow the seed, and you begin to use what you have been given the way you ought to, then you will create everything you have been promised.

2. Be Word Conscious

A man's belly shall be satisfied from the fruits of his mouth, and from the produce of the increase of his lips shall he be filled. Death and life are in the power of the tongue, and they that love it shall eat the fruits.2

Words are seeds3 and they produce fruits. That is the reason you must speak positively. To speak positively does not mean auto-suggestion; it means to make divinely-inspired statements about your life, business or your future. Speak it every day when you wake up in the morning. Declare your dreams; "I'm a blessing to humanity, a breath of fresh air to mankind."

3. Work!

Grace does not operate in a vacuum. Success is the grace of God appropriated by the effort of man. There must be something you are doing and steps you are taking. Things will not happen just because you wished for them. Whatever you do not work at, does not work out.

Everything remains in the state of rest or uniform motion until a greater force is applied! Now consider how much you have today. Not how much you earn alone, but how much you have. Consider how much you will like to have or how much you will like to be worth in the next twelve months. Ask yourself, 'if I keep doing what I'm doing now, will it give me that kind of result?' To keep doing the same things and expecting different results is the definition of insanity. Something is wrong somewhere! For change to occur, a greater force has to be applied.

4. Be Grateful

Gratitude is a proof that a man has not lost his memory. It is an attitude that opens the heavens for greater increase and keeps it open. We may not celebrate arrival, but we should be grateful for progress. You need to find things that are working despite the ones that are not yet working and be grateful for them. As you begin to appreciate Him and to count your blessings, you won't stop counting them, because the things that you count never stop to count.

5. Stretch!

Every time you set a goal, you create a distance between where you are and where you would rather be. Once you recognize there is a distance, there will be a sense of compulsion to want to cover that distance. But when there are no goals, there is no motivation to aspire to reach them.

The credible, authentic way to keep rising is by making a commitment to exceptional performance in whatever it is you are doing. So, stretch and set goals. You've got to have goals that are beyond your current means.
If you have goals beyond your means, then you will know you need to stretch beyond your reach.

A man will never rise if he does only what he's assigned to do. Promotion only comes through exceptional performance. A promotion that cannot be traced back to competence can never be sustained. That is not a real lifting. Every authentic promotion comes from within the ambit of true competence.

6. Ditch Your Limits!

For many years in the field of athletic events, they said it was not possible for anybody to run one mile in less than four minutes. Everybody believed it. So they never stretched beyond it until a man called Roger Bannister came and broke that record.

You know what happened? The moment Roger Bannister broke that record, everybody began to break the record. Today, even ordinary children who don't have to go through any special training are breaking that record. So what happened before then? Some people set a ceiling; some people created a mental barrier. And they said 'this is not possible'.

And there are many things people have said it's not possible that have become possible.

A man once said that if God wanted man to fly, he would have made him a bird with wings or at least given him wings to fly like angels. That sounded very intelligent, but are human beings not "flying" now?

7. Be Careful Who You Are Listening To

Based on the law of aerodynamics, a bumble bee should never be able to fly, but the bumble bee does not know the law of aerodynamics. So the bumble bee is flying. The bumble bee never went to a school of aerodynamics where they would have told her about her limitation.

A teacher once came out into an exam room and said to the students, "You can answer all the questions, but don't try question four. You may try it, if you have the time, but nobody has ever solved question four before. So don't waste your time on it; try the other questions."

When the result came out, nobody had attempted question four except one young man and he got it right! The lecturer, surprised said, "How did you do it? Didn't you hear when I said nobody has ever solved question four?" The young man said "No sir. I came late. I got to the exam hall after the announcement. I did not hear when you said nobody has ever solved question four." Thank God he did not hear. If he heard, the same barrier would have been placed on his mind.

8. Celebrate milestones, but keep moving

Life is not an endless race that just goes on. Life is to be occasioned by milestones with scheduled rest intervals in between. You are not on the run permanently, neither are you resting endlessly.

'Let us run with patience...' 4 is the paradigm for life. Set goals, achieve them, and celebrate the success.

After that, be renewed and refreshed and then move on.

It's recommended in most organizations to go on a break in December. In fact, in many countries, firms shut down their operations in December, because to go from January to December without any rest doesn't make it look like twelve months any more. The first month of the New Year now looks like the thirteenth month, and the law of diminishing returns begins to set in. Motivation is low, because you are just working ceaselessly.

If you are on the run permanently, you will eventually burn out and if you are resting endlessly, you will gradually grow stale. So, it is wisdom to know the balance.

I am more than convinced, that our enlightened present will no longer be subservient to our ignorant past.

Welcome to unending success!

A WORD FOR THE UNSAVED

Denying the existence of God is the highest level of folly. A book is a proof of the existence of an author; a poem proves the existence of a poet. The world is too orderly for a man to assume he came out of nothing. This God did not just make the earth; someday we will stand before him in judgment. Jesus remains the only way to Him. He did not say "I am a way…" Rather, He said "I am the way…" If He had said He was a way, we would have been left with options. Dear friend, we only have one option – Jesus. He remains the only guarantee for lasting success!

ABOUT THE AUTHOR

GBEMINIYI EBODA is the convener and host of the life changing conference "Move Your World" where he teaches upward mobility strategies and principles required to move from a life of survival to that of success and significance.

He is in high demand as a teacher and preacher of God's word, human capital trainer and in church capacity building operations.

He sits as president of Ecclesia Consulting and Senior Pastor of HarvestHouse Christian Center with branches in Nigeria, United Kingdom, Ghana and South Africa.

OTHER TITLES BY THE AUTHOR

YOU ARE MORE THAN THIS

There's no barrier to success. It's all about you. This book will help you find a way out of ignorance and develop a very strong database that will usher you into the future that you have always dreamt of.

BECOMING A MONEY MAGNET

There's money everywhere! But it is only within the reach of those who will dare to reach out for it. A copy of this book will empower your mind with principles of financial intelligence.

ACHIEVERS' GOLDMINE

You are the main character in this book! This text is a blue-print or guide which if followed will take you from where you are to where you want and passionately desire to be in life and the whole concept is to help unearth the value on your inside from its potential form.

OTHER TITLES BY THE AUTHOR

YOUR DESTINY IS IN YOUR COMPETENCE

This text is another archetypal to guide you from living a life of activity into a life of higher productivity!

ORACLES OF WISDOM

In this book are wisdom nuggets covering different aspects of life. It's a mini book for a mega life!

SINGLE WITHOUT WRINKLES

A toast to every spinster, the truth for every bachelor. This book is God's wisdom delicately packaged for the lady to disentangle her from the web of influences and past experiences hindering her from being maximised.

OTHER TITLES BY THE AUTHOR

DARE TO EXCEL
Success requires that you believe in God, yourself and the dream. These are wisdom tips packaged for a forward-focused dreamer on his way to achieving greatness.

www.ingramcontent.com/pod-product-compliance
Lightning Source LLC
Chambersburg PA
CBHW031448040426
42444CB00007B/1027